TARANTULAS

TARANTULAS

Written and illustrated by

JOAN BERG VICTOR

DODD, MEAD & COMPANY, NEW YORK

ACKNOWLEDGMENTS

A great thank you to Alice Gray and Arthur Bordes for all their knowledge.

Library of Congress Cataloging in Publication Data

Victor, Joan Berg.
Tarantulas.

Includes index.
SUMMARY: Text and drawings focus on the senses,
mating, young, molting, silk, and homes of the hairy,
primitive spiders reputed to be very dangerous.
1. Tarantulas—Juvenile literature.
[1. Tarantulas. 2. Spiders] I. Title.
QL458.42.T5V52   595'.44   78–11548
ISBN 0–396–07639–4

To my parents
and
to my children, Danny and Lizzie

TARANTULAS

Tarantulas are primitive spiders. Because of the way they look—usually brown or black and hairy all over and measuring up to ten inches when the legs are outstretched—tarantulas have the reputation of being very dangerous. The truth is that they are rather sluggish and attack only when extremely provoked. A few can give a painful bite. There are eighty to ninety species of tarantulas in the southern United States.

All spiders belong to the class Arachnida. They have hard external skeletons and four pairs of jointed legs. They have no antennae and no wings. There are true, or advanced, spiders and there are the primitive spiders, the tarantulas.

Tarantulas existed before the dinosaurs. Over the millions of years, they have changed very little from their prehistoric ancestors. True spiders have changed or adapted themselves over the years. Differences in their lungs, spinnerets, and eyes separate the primitive spiders from the true spiders.

LUNGS

All tarantulas have two pairs of book lungs, which are used for breathing. They are called "book lungs" because they look like the pages of a book, bound on one side. The book lungs of the tarantulas appear as four openings along the sides of the abdomen.

Book lungs

Because true spiders lead more active lives, they need a more efficient breathing system. They breathe by means of one pair of book lungs and a system of tracheae, or air tubes.

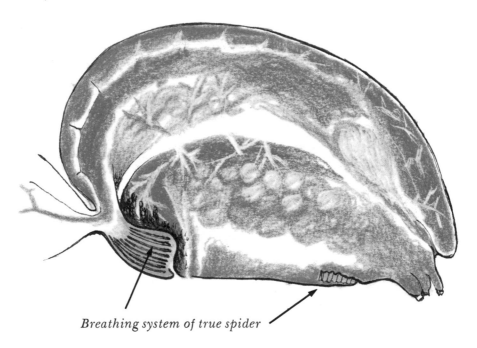

Breathing system of true spider

SILK AND SPINNING
All spiders, including the tarantulas, spin silk. The word spider comes from the Anglo-Saxon word "spinnan" meaning "to spin."

Spinnerets

    Silk was originally a waste product of the spider. Spiders have specialized organs called spinnerets which produce silk. Each spinneret and each pore opening on the spinneret produces a different kind of silk used for a particular purpose.

Prey trapped in spider's web

True spiders have three or four pairs of spinnerets, and depend on silk far more than tarantulas do. True spiders use silk as a bridge, a swing, a lasso, for cocoons, nests, webs for trapping food, and for ballooning from one place to another. Young spiders, because of their lightness, are able to climb to high points, let out their silk, and away they go—traveling great distances on the silk. This distributes spiders to various areas.

Young spider ballooning

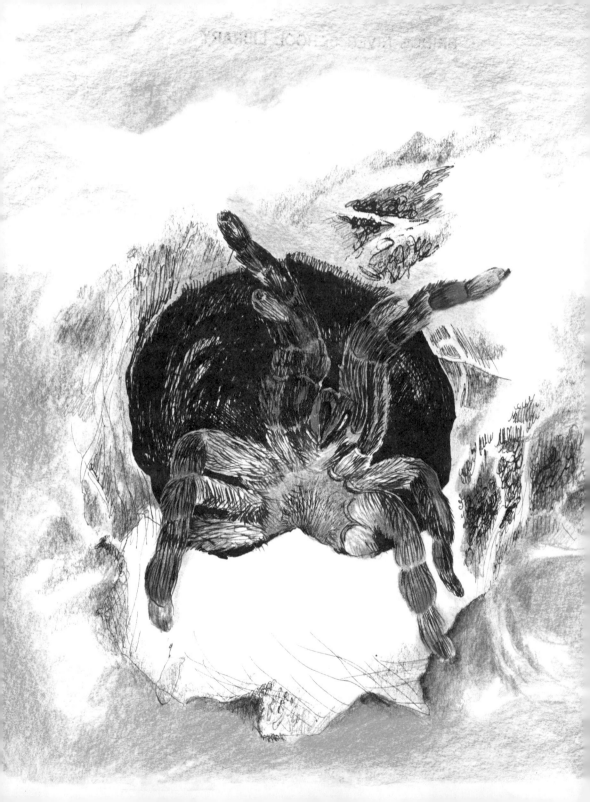

Tarantulas have only two pairs of spinnerets. (The second pair is so small it can hardly be seen.) Their use of silk is limited mainly for lining nests and for egg cases. They never learned to use silk to trap prey, and it was only by accident that it became a help in capturing their food. Using silk to trap prey came about when they were lining their nests with silk and some spilled over on the ground. The vibration of an insect walking on this silk "doormat" could be felt within the nest. The vibration on the silk became a signal that food was nearby.

SENSES

Tarantulas have eight eyes, all crowded together in one bump on the top of their heads. True spiders have eight, six, four, or two eyes, depending on the particular species. Even though they have eight eyes, tarantulas are almost blind and can see only light and dark because their eyes are not well developed. They survive mainly by their sense of touch. Food must come to them, and although they strike at their prey with great speed, they are not very accurate.

Close-up of eyes

Tarantulas do not have ears and probably cannot hear. Most of the hairs on their bodies act as sense organs. Some are used to feel vibrations. Some, in the mouth, are used for taste. Some, perhaps, are used to smell with. There are hairs on the abdomen which tarantulas throw off in combat. These hairs are not poisonous, but they do cause an irritation or a distraction for enemies.

The Wolf Spider

The American tarantulas are not the same as what is called a tarantula in Europe. The European tarantula is really a wolf spider. It is not poisonous, and it is not a primitive spider like our tarantulas. The Italian dance "tarantella" was thought for centuries to have been danced to cure the bite of a tarantula—used as a means of getting the poison out of the system. But, this was probably only an excuse to have an otherwise not-allowed street dance.

Wolf spider

Black widow spider

The really fatally poisonous spiders of the world are not tarantulas. Only the black widow spider and its relatives are poisonous, and these are true spiders.

HOMES

Most tarantulas are ground-loving spiders, although some of them live in cracks in trees or under stones. They dig their own burrows or move into those abandoned by other tarantulas or rodents, and remodel the hole to suit their needs. When a tarantula grows too big for its burrow, it just enlarges it by cutting away bits of soil or pebbles with its rakelike fangs.

All spiders, including tarantulas, need water to drink, but more than a few drops will cause them to flee their burrows. Flooding is a great danger to tarantulas.

Tarantulas remain in their burrows most of the time, venturing out only for food. The male tarantulas, when they mature, wander about looking for mates.

Food

Tarantulas eat all kinds of beetles—especially ground beetles and June beetles. Beetles seem to contain an ingredient necessary for the females to reproduce. Tarantulas also eat grasshoppers and caterpillars.

They use their fangs like straws for eating, injecting a substance which liquifies the food, enabling the tarantulas to suck up the food. Only a pellet of skeleton remains of a victim.

Fangs

Tarantulas can live for long periods without food, and in winter they take no food at all. They must have water though. If they have been without water for a while, they will shrink. If placed in a dish of water, they will appear to grow like a sponge.

LIFESPAN

The lifespan of tarantulas varies greatly. North American tarantulas—those that live in moderate climates—live longer than tropical ones.

In the case of some North American tarantulas that have been kept in captivity, females have lived to be twenty-five years of age. Tropical female tarantulas in captivity have been known to live up to seven years, reaching maturity at three years.

A male tarantula lives only six months to a year after he becomes mature. In North American tarantulas, this occurs when he is about ten years old. Until that time, the immature males and females look alike and both live in burrows in the ground.

Molting

Young tarantulas "molt" or shed their entire exo-
skeletons three times a year. With each molt,
tarantulas grow a bit. If they have lost a leg, they
will grow a new one. After four or five years, they
molt only twice a year. Before shedding, the tarantula stops eating, turns on its back, and remains
almost immobile. The molting takes an hour or
an hour and fifteen minutes, and as it molts the
tarantula appears to be rising up and out of its
skin.

*Empty exoskeleton
after molting*

All tarantulas have a black spot on their abdomens, which they are born with and which stays until they are about seven years old.

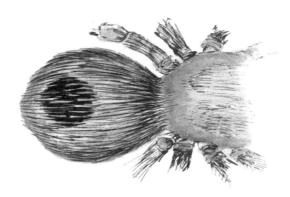

At the age of ten years, when the male has shed his skin for the last time, it is possible to tell the male from the female. He is now darker than the female, being almost black with a few brown hairs. He is also smaller than the female.

Hooks under the two front legs and enlarged tips exist only in the male.

A female tarantula continues to shed her skin once a year for her entire lifetime—each time growing a tiny bit.

Female shedding skin

MATURITY AND MATING

Only female tarantulas continue to molt after maturity and only the females acquire a new dark brown coat.

Tarantulas get a complete new set of hairs each time they molt, so if they lost most of them in trying to catch prey or ward off enemies, they are replaced. By molting, the tarantula's body stays young.

The male tarantula does not live long enough to shed after maturity. After the last molt, the mature male tarantula becomes a wanderer. He is no longer content to live alone in his burrow underground. He may wander for miles in search of a mate. All the males of a certain area seem to go in the same direction, like birds migrating.

Whether or not they find mates, the males will die within the year, if not from courtship or in combat, then just from old age. They will just eventually stop eating and drinking, their spinnerets will fall off, and they will die.

The female tarantula often uses the same burrow for her entire life.

Between the time she becomes mature and the time she dies at about twenty-five years she will mate perhaps several times a year, early in October, and each litter will have several hundred to a thousand baby tarantulas. Although she mates in the fall, she does not lay her eggs until June.

Males looking for mates

Female spinning cocoon

Young

The female tarantula will spin a cocoon in which to place her eggs. In most cases, the cocoon will be at the opening of the burrow, usually in a partially concealed place, perhaps behind a stone. Only a few tarantulas have a burrow large enough to spin the cocoon within.

The spinning of the cocoon will take about fifteen hours to finish. As the hours go by, she works less, rests more, and when she finally finishes, she lays her eggs in a yellow liquid on the silk hammock she has spun. Then she rapidly spins again, this time to make a cover.

When she has finished, she pulls up the edges, rolls the whole sac up, turns it over, and sits on it. For six weeks, she watches over the sac, ready to defend it. She keeps one or two feet on the cocoon at all times. The only insects she cannot defend against are ants—they will attack the cocoon and eat the eggs.

Female sitting on egg sac

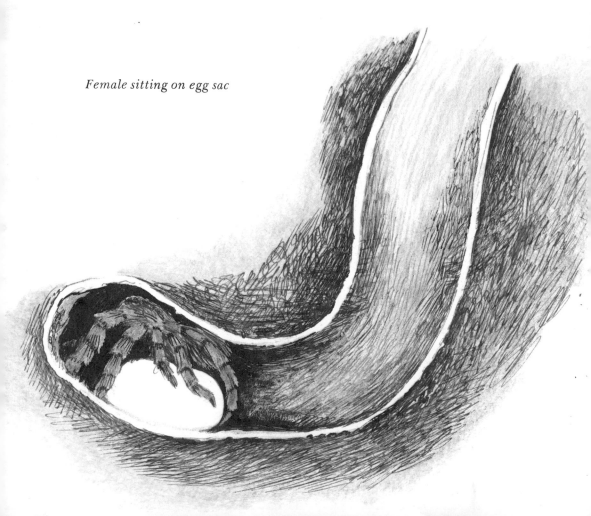

After three weeks, the young tarantulas hatch from their eggs. They remain in the cocoon, though, sometimes for several months. When ready, they make little round holes and crawl out. Some tarantulas are not fully grown when they come out of the cocoon, and the mother and babies weave a nursery web where they stay for a week or so. After a week the babies will shed their first skin.

Nursery web

Baby tree tarantula

The young remain around the mother tarantula for four to fifteen days and then go off on their own. They take no food until the following spring, and by summer only about fifteen of the entire litter will have survived.

When the female reaches the end of her life, she has difficulty in sloughing off her exoskeleton. This difficulty in molting shows the age of the tarantula.

CURIOUS HOMES AND THEIR BUILDERS

Some scientists consider the trapdoor, purse-web, and the funnel-web spiders as tarantulas. Others believe they are merely related. Whatever the classification, these spiders build some curious and interesting homes.

TRAPDOOR SPIDERS

These are the best tunnel-makers and the inventors of the trapdoor which is used for defense.

Trapdoor spider

There are three kinds of trapdoors:

Cork nest—This is a simple tunnel house, which is lined with silk, and has a door which fits like a cork.

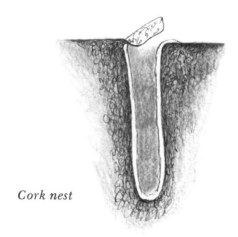

Cork nest

Wafer door—Another simple tunnel house lined with silk, with a thin wafer door closing the entrance. This wafer is covered with leaves and sticks as a camouflage.

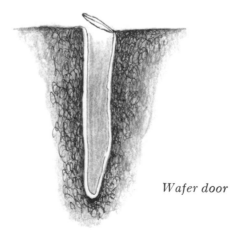

Wafer door

Double-doored—This tunnel is lined with silk also, and has a side tunnel closed off by a second trapdoor.

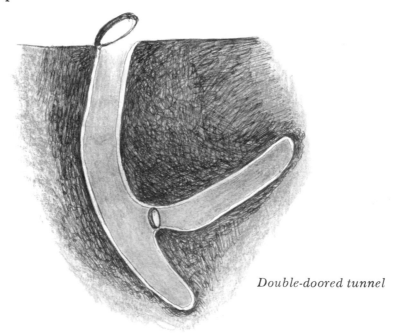

Double-doored tunnel

The trapdoor burrows are roomy. One spider lives alone, away from sun, water, extreme cold or heat, and can easily be hidden. It keeps out its enemies by holding the door shut with its claws with great force, hides the door with camouflage, and sometimes builds an additional tunnel.

At night, the spider sits with the door a little open, looking out. When a victim comes close, the spider grabs it. The trapdoor spider lays eggs inside the silk-lined tunnel. The eggs are hatched, and the babies remain for several weeks.

Purse-web spider

PURSE-WEB SPIDERS

These are very small tarantulas, only about ¾″ long. They make a hole in the ground, perhaps two feet deep. They line this tunnel with silk and continue to weave silk outside the nest into a long tube.

When an insect walks on the tube, it causes a vibration. The spider runs up the tube from its burrow, cuts a hole in the silk, and grabs its victim.

The purse-web tube usually leans against a tree trunk.

FUNNEL-WEB SPIDERS

Their tunnels are wider at the mouth, with a silk sheet extending from the door. This sheet forms a funnel, and the spider waits for insects to get caught in it, then rushes to catch its prey.

Funnel web

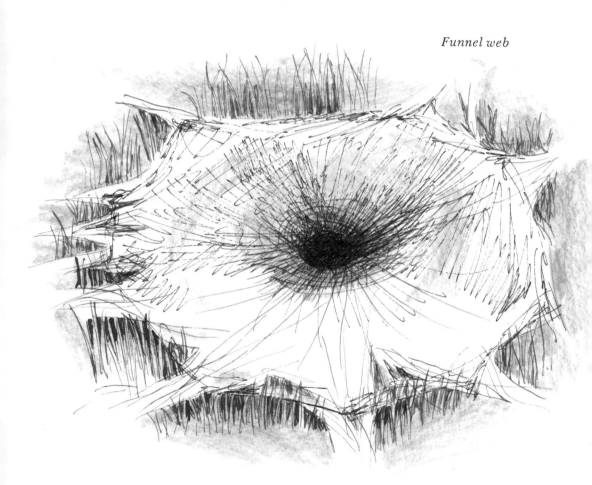

Sheet web

SHEET-WEB SPIDERS

These catch their prey in a manner similar to the funnel-web spiders, spinning a wide silk sheet from the opening of its nest. They have the best eyesight of all tarantulas.

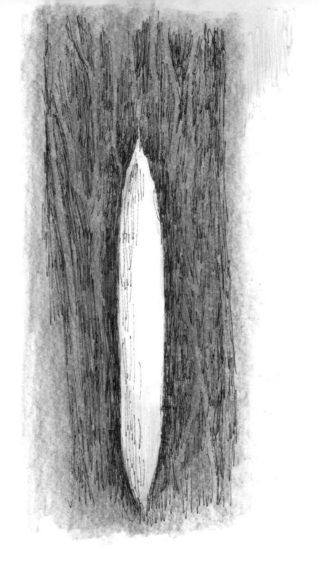

Tree Tarantulas

These construct a silk tube high in a tree. When an insect lands on its tube, the tarantula makes a hole and pulls the victim inside.

44

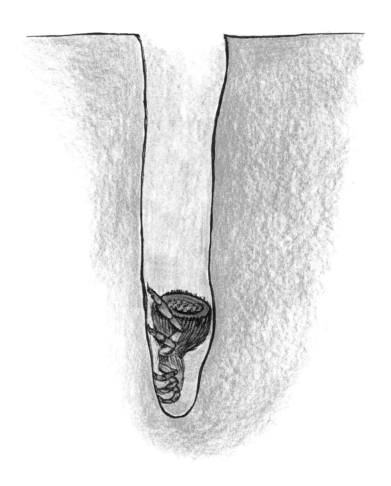

Mygalae Truncata

This means "cut-off short" and this spider lives in a hole without a silk lining. Instead of a door, it uses a hard disk on the end of its rear as a door.

INTERESTING FACTS ABOUT TARANTULAS

The largest of all the tarantulas live in the hot jungles of Brazil. They can have a body length of three and a half inches, or as large as a dinner plate. These are often called bird-eating tarantulas and have been known to eat small birds.

Many tarantulas from the tropics live in trees. They are able to jump great distances when disturbed. These tarantulas build a saclike web which they use as a retreat when molting.

A tree tarantula of Trinidad has pink legs and a black body and black feet when young. In the adult, the colors are reversed.

The baboon tarantula, so-called because of its bright red hair, is aggressive and one is known to have chased a dog from a room. It was also known to have eaten a mouse completely.

The hairs on many tarantulas can cause itching and sneezing and sometimes a rash. This is to drive animals away that might want to harm them.

The long-hair tarantula is able to jump from heights, using its hairs like a parachute.

CLASSIFICATION OF TARANTULAS

ANIMAL KINGDOM
Phylum—Arthropoda
Class—Arachnida
Order—Araneae
Suborder—Mygalomorphae

INDEX

Arachnida (class), 10

Bite, 9
Black spot, 28
Black widow spider, 21
Book lungs, 11–12

Classification, 47
Cocoon, 32–34, 35
Color, 9, 28, 29, 46

Exoskeleton, 10, 27, 36

Feeding, 24–25, 36, 40, 41, 42, 43, 44, 46
Flooding, 22
Funnel-web spider, 37, 42

Homes, 22, 32, 37, 38, 39, 40, 41, 42, 43, 44, 45, 46

Legs, 10
Lifespan, 26

Mating, 29–30
Migration, 30
Molting, 27–29, 30
Mygalae truncata, 45

Nursery web, 35

Purse-web spider, 37, 41

Senses, 18–19
  eyes, 18, 19, 43
  hairs, 19, 29, 47
Sheet-web spider, 43
Silk, 12–13, 15, 17
  uses, 17, 32–34, 35, 38, 39, 40, 41, 46
Size, 9, 28–29, 46
Species, 9
Spinnerets, 13, 15, 17

Tarantulas
  differences from true spiders, 10–19
Trapdoor spiders, 37–40
  cork nest, 38
  double-doored nest, 39
  wafer nest, 38
Tree tarantula, 44
True spiders, 10, 12, 15, 18

Water, 22
Wolf spider, 20

Young, 30, 31–36